MARVELS ANIMALS 28

SEALS

QUINN M. ARNOLD

CREATIVE EDUCATION | CREATIVE PAPERBACKS

table of contents

Greetings, Seals!.................... 1

Warm in the Water................. 7

Molting Fur...................... 10

Time to Eat!..................... 12

Seal Pups...................... 14

What Do Seals Do?.............. 16

Farewell, Seals!................. 18

Picture a Seal................... 20

Words to Know................. 22

Read More..................... 22

Websites....................... 22

Index.......................... 24

Published by Creative Education and Creative Paperbacks
P.O. Box 227, Mankato, Minnesota 56002
Creative Education and Creative Paperbacks
are imprints of The Creative Company
www.thecreativecompany.us

Design by Graham Morgan
Art direction by Blue Design (www.bluedes.com)

Images by Alamy/Doug Allan, 6–7, Poelzer Wolfgang, 13; Dreamstime/ Isselee, cover (right), 3, 20–21, 24, Izanbar, 23, Lynn Bystrom, cover (middle), 1; Getty Images/David Madison, 2; Pexels/Chen Te, cover (left), 18–19, Elianne Dipp, 16; Public Domain/Biodiversity Heritage Library, 4; Shutterstock/Michael A. Damanski, 10–11, Ondrej Prosicky, 8–9, Philip Ellard, 17; Wikimedia Commons/Alastair Rae, 14–15

Copyright © 2025 Creative Education, Creative Paperbacks
International copyright reserved in all countries.
No part of this book may be reproduced in any form
without written permission from the publisher.

Library of Congress Cataloging-in-Publication Data
Names: Arnold, Quinn M., author.
Title: Seals / by Quinn M. Arnold.
Description: Mankato, Minnesota : Creative Education and Creative Paperbacks, [2025] | Series: Marvels | Revised edition of: Seals / Quinn M. Arnold. [2017]. | Includes bibliographical references and index. | Audience: Ages 4–7 | Audience: Grades K–1 | Summary: "An introduction to seals, this beginning reader features eye-catching photographs, humorous captions, and basic life science facts about these sleek ocean mammals. Includes a labeled image guide, glossary, and further resources"— Provided by publisher.
Identifiers: LCCN 2024014649 (print) | LCCN 2024014650 (ebook) | ISBN 9798889892243 (library binding) | ISBN 9781682775905 (paperback) | ISBN 9798889893356 (ebook)
Subjects: LCSH: Seals (Animals)—Juvenile literature. | Animals—Juvenile literature. | CYAC: Seals (Animals). | Animals.
Classification: LCC QL737.P64 A76 2025 (print) | LCC QL737.P64 (ebook) | DDC 599.79--dc23/eng/20240422
LC record available at https://lccn.loc.gov/2024014649
LC ebook record available at https://lccn.loc.gov/2024014650

Printed in China

Seals live in **oceans**. Thick **blubber** keeps seals warm.

A seal's back **flippers** help it swim fast. A seal on land is slow. Its claws dig into rocks and ice.

Many seals have dark brown or gray fur. Some have spots. Seals molt every year.

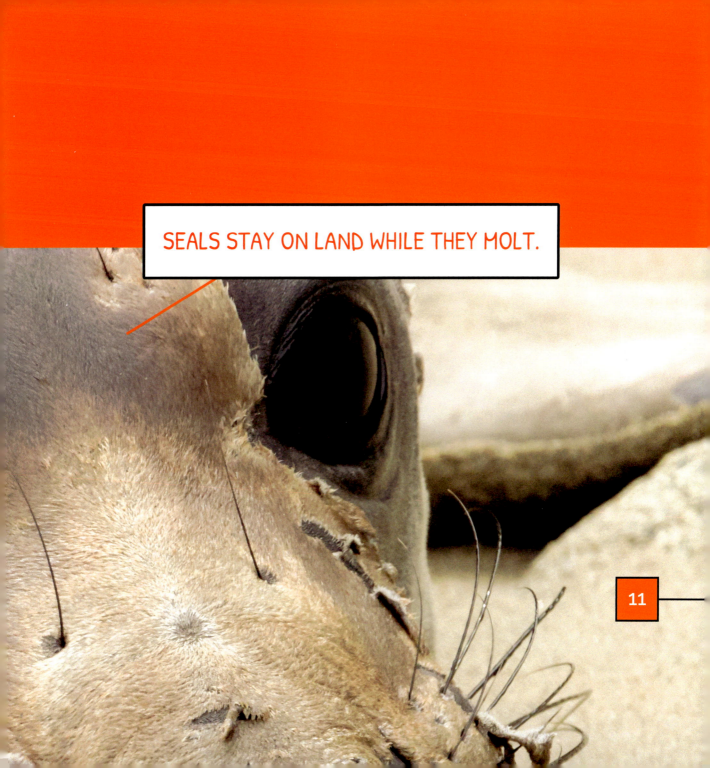

Big-eyed seals look for food. They eat a lot of fish. Some seals eat squid or octopuses, too.

Many seals spend half their life on land.

Baby seals are called pups. They are born on land. Pups learn to swim. Then they look for food alone.

Seals rest on land. They swim in the oceans. They dive deep for food.

[Picture a Seal]

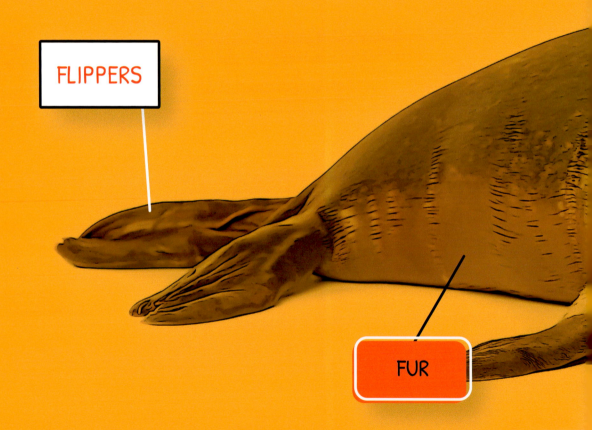

20

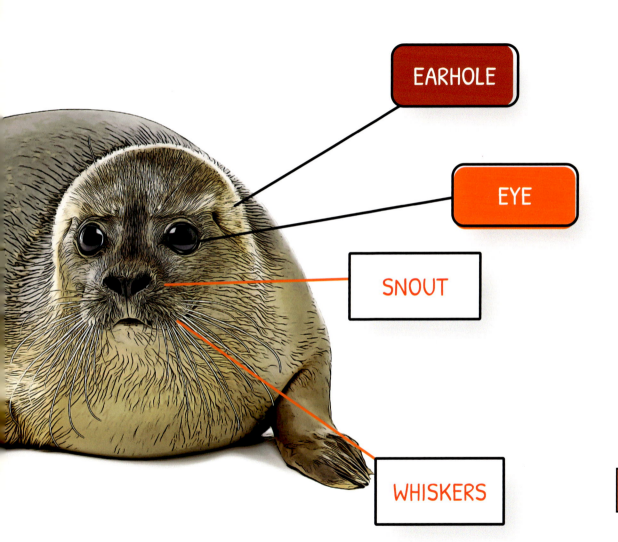

WORDS TO KNOW

blubber: a thick layer of fat that keeps ocean animals warm

flipper: a flat limb (like an arm) that helps a seal swim

molt: to lose and regrow hair or skin

ocean: a big area of deep, salty water

READ MORE

Bolte, Mari. *I am Not a Penguin: Animals in the Polar Regions*. North Mankato, Minn.: Pebble, an imprint of Capstone, 2022.

Miller, Debbie S. *Glaciers are Alive*. Watertown, Mass.: Charlesbridge, 2023.

WEBSITES

National Geographic Kids: Harp Seal
https://kids.nationalgeographic.com/animals/mammals/facts/harp-seal

Find out about harp seals and how they live in the chilly Arctic.

Seal Sitters
https://www.sealsitters.org/marine_mammals/kidstuff.html

Facts, activities, and ideas on how to help seals in the wild.

INDEX

blubber, 7
claws, 9
eyes, 12, 21
flippers, 9, 20
food, 12, 15, 16
fur, 10, 20
molting, 10, 11
pups, 15
swimming, 9, 15, 16